Shapes

Written and Compiled by **Elizabeth McKinnon**
Illustrated by **Reg Sandland**

Totline® Publications
A Division of Frank Schaffer Publications, Inc.
Torrance, California

Totline Publications would like to thank the following people for their contributions to this book: Barbara Backer, Charleston, SC; Ellen Javernick, Loveland, CO; Kathy McCullough, St. Charles, IL; Lois E. Putnam, Pilot Mountain, NC; Jacki Smallwood, Royersford, PA.

Managing Editor: Kathleen Cubley
Contributing Editors: Carol Gnojewski, Susan Hodges, Susan Sexton, Jean Warren
Copyeditor: Kris Fulsaas
Proofreader: Miriam Bulmer
Editorial Assistant: Durby Peterson
Graphic Designer: Sarah Ness
Graphic Designer (Cover): Brenda Mann Harrison
Cover Illustrator: Kelly McMahon
Production Manager: Melody Olney

Some of the ideas in this book may appear in other Totline® publications.

ISBN: 1-57029-197-7

Printed in the United States of America
Published by Totline® Publications
Editorial Office: P.O. Box 2250
Everett, WA 98203
Business Office: 23740 Hawthorne Blvd.
Torrance, CA 90505

20 19 18 17 16 15 14 13 12 11 10 9 8 7 6 5 4 3 2 1

Introduction

Recognizing basic shapes, such as circles, squares, and triangles, is an important step in the development of young children's math skills.

A quick glance around your house will reveal that shapes are everywhere, making it easy for you to help your child learn the shape-recognition skills he or she needs.

Shapes opens with the chapter "Basic Shapes." This chapter is made up of activities to help develop your child's understanding of circles, squares, triangles, rectangles, ovals, diamonds, hearts, and stars.

The second chapter, "Shape Review," contains activities designed for working with any shape as well as with more than one shape.

Young children learn best when they engage in various kinds of activities that allow them to play, explore, and discover. To provide for this, the activities in *Shapes* include suggestions for language, art, learning games, music and movement, science, and snacks.

As you work with the ideas in *Shapes,* we hope that you will find them to be useful. If your child has difficulty with an activity, feel free to adapt it or to try another one you feel is more suitable. Most importantly, keep in mind that your child will learn best when he or she is having fun.

A Word About Safety—All the activities in this book are appropriate for children ages 3 to 5. However, it is important that an adult supervise the activities to make sure that children do not put any materials or objects in their mouth. As for art materials, such as scissors, glue, or felt tip markers, use those that are specifically labeled as safe for children unless the materials are to be used only by an adult.

Contents

Coin Puzzle

Using coins is a fun way to help your child recognize the circle shape.

You Will Need

- ❑ penny
- ❑ nickel
- ❑ dime
- ❑ quarter
- ❑ heavy paper
- ❑ pen
- ❑ coin purse or small box

Make a gameboard by arranging a penny, a nickel, a dime, and a quarter on a piece of heavy paper and using a pen to trace around each one. Remove the coins and place them in a coin purse or a small box. To play, sit with your child and give him the purse or box of coins. Point out the four different sizes of circles on the gameboard. Ask your child to take one of the coins from the purse and move it around on the gameboard until he finds the matching-sized circle. Invite him to continue in the same way with the remaining coins. When all the coins are on the gameboard, talk about their appearance. How are the coins different? How are their shapes the same?

For Older Kids: Make the game more challenging by using more than one of each coin.

Circle Prints

Let your child help you look around the house for small, round objects that can be used for printing circles, such as corks, spools, short cardboard tubes, bottle caps, and small jar lids. Set out the objects along with paper and colored ink pads. Have your child press the round objects onto the ink pads and then stamp them onto the paper any way she wishes to make circle prints. Encourage her to talk about the sizes and colors of the prints as she creates her own unique circle designs. When she has finished, display her artwork where she can easily see it.

This art activity allows your child to experience making circles of several different sizes.

You Will Need

- ❑ small, round objects for printing circles
- ❑ paper
- ❑ ink pads

Square Sandwich Puzzle

This tasty puzzle promotes recognition of the square shape.

You Will Need

- ❑ bread
- ❑ knife
- ❑ sandwich filling
- ❑ plate

At lunchtime, turn two slices of bread into squares by trimming off the edges. Spread on a firm sandwich filling, such as peanut butter, put the bread squares together, then cut the sandwich into four smaller squares. Place the sandwich pieces at random on a plate. Talk with your child about the square shape of each sandwich piece. Then invite him to put the four small squares together to make a larger square before he enjoys his "puzzle sandwich."

Craft Stick Square

Give your child four identical craft sticks. Help her see that the sticks are all the same length by encouraging her to put them together in various ways. Explain that a square has four sides that are all the same length. Then help her arrange and glue the sticks in a square shape, as shown in the illustration. When the glue has dried, invite your child to decorate her square with colored glue, paint, or marker designs. Then tie a piece of yarn to the square and hang it on a wall or a door.

With this art activity, a constructed square becomes a creative wall decoration.

You Will Need

- ❑ craft sticks
- ❑ glue
- ❑ colored glue, paint, or markers
- ❑ yarn

Making Triangles

Your child makes his own triangles for this learning activity.

You Will Need

- ❑ child-safe scissors
- ❑ ruler
- ❑ construction paper
- ❑ large piece of paper
- ❑ glue

Cut 2- to 3-inch squares out of various colors of construction paper. Talk with your child about the shapes of the squares. Then help him fold the squares in half diagonally and cut along the fold to make triangles. Ask him to count the number of sides and points on each shape. Cut a large piece of paper, such as brown wrapping paper, into a large triangle. Then let your child glue his smaller triangles onto the large triangle any way he wishes.

Complete the Triangles

Sit with your child at a table. At the top of a piece of paper, use a marker to draw several small triangles. Ask your child to count the number of points and sides each one has. Then draw several large triangles on the paper, leaving off a different side on each one. Give the marker to your child and invite her to draw a line to complete each triangle shape. Then let her decorate her completed triangles with crayons.

This learning game helps reinforce the concept that triangles have three sides.

You Will Need

- ❑ paper
- ❑ marker
- ❑ crayons

Frame-Ups

This activity lets your child work with various sizes of rectangles.

You Will Need

- ❑ three sizes of index cards
- ❑ ruler
- ❑ craft knife
- ❑ crayons or markers

Select three index cards of different sizes. Use a ruler and a craft knife to cut out a rectangle, in one piece, from the center of each card. Set aside the three outer "frames." Give the rectangles to your child and let him decorate the shapes with crayons or markers to make pictures for the frames. As he works, talk about how each rectangle has two long sides and two short sides. When he has finished, set out the three frames. Then invite your child to match his pictures to the frames so that all three pictures are visible.

Postcard Puzzles

Collect four or five rectangular picture postcards. Use scissors to cut each card into several interlocking pieces to make a simple puzzle. Store each puzzle in a small, resealable plastic bag. To play, sit with your child at a table or on the floor and give her one of the puzzle bags. Have her remove the pieces and put them together to complete the puzzle. Call attention to the rectangle shape of the puzzle when it is completed and ask your child to point to the two long sides, then the two short sides. Then let her select other postcard puzzles to put together.

For Older Kids: Cut each card into a larger number of pieces. Or, mix the pieces of two or three puzzles together and store them in the same bag.

Picture postcards are great to use for developing recognition of the rectangle shape.

You Will Need

- ❑ picture postcards
- ❑ scissors
- ❑ resealable plastic bags

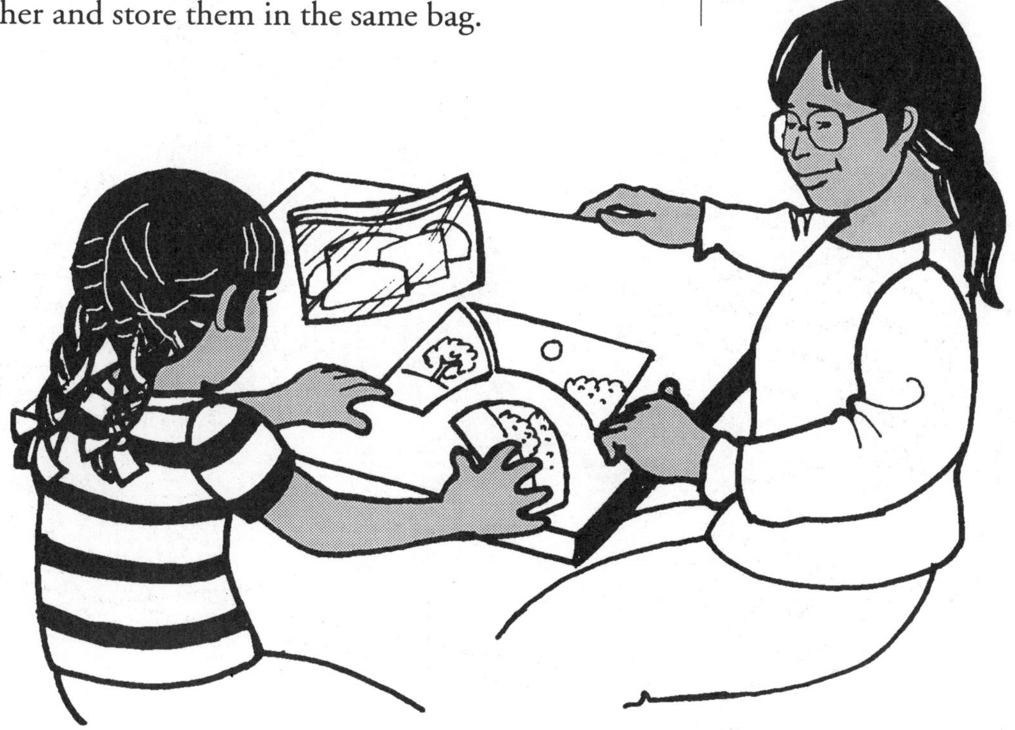

Oval Egg Game

This homemade sorting game gives your child practice in recognizing the oval shape.

You Will Need

- ❑ white construction paper
- ❑ scissors
- ❑ ruler
- ❑ shoebox with lid
- ❑ egg-carton half

From white construction paper, cut out six oval shapes about 2½ inches tall by 1½ inches wide. Also cut out six to eight other small shapes such as circles, squares, and triangles. Place all the shapes in a shoebox and set out an empty egg-carton half. Show your child one of the ovals and point out how it looks like an egg. Put the shape back into the shoebox and mix all the shapes together. Then have your child sort through the shapes to find the oval "eggs" and place them in the cups of the egg-carton half. Store the shapes and the egg-carton half inside the shoebox for your child to play with again whenever he wishes.

Bean Ovals

Use a crayon to draw three different sizes of ovals on a piece of construction paper. Set out a small container of glue, a paintbrush, and a bowl of oval-shaped dried beans. Sit with your child and show her the paper with the ovals drawn on it. Talk about the oval shapes and compare them with the shapes of the dried beans. Then invite her to brush glue on the paper and arrange the beans on top of the glue, in and around the ovals, any way she wishes. (Remember to closely supervise any activity that uses small objects such as dried beans.)

For Older Kids: Encourage children to glue beans around the oval outlines or to create patterns with the various dried beans.

Reinforce understanding of the oval shape with this art activity.

You Will Need

- ❑ crayon
- ❑ construction paper
- ❑ small container
- ❑ glue
- ❑ paintbrush
- ❑ bowl
- ❑ oval-shaped dried beans

Playing-Card Diamonds

Here's a new use for an old deck of playing cards.

You Will Need

- ❑ pen
- ❑ paper
- ❑ deck of playing cards

Draw a diamond shape on a piece of paper and talk about the shape with your child. Have him count the number of sides and the number of points on the shape. Then from an old deck of playing cards, select the diamond and heart cards from 2 to 10. (Discard the face cards.) Mix up the diamond and heart cards and invite your child to sort out the ones that have diamonds on them. Help him arrange the cards in order from 2 to 10. Then, on each card, have him point to the diamonds one by one as you count them together.

Diamond Kite

From white paper, cut out a diamond shape about 7 inches tall. Fold the shape in half lengthwise and give it to your child. When she unfolds the paper, talk about its diamond shape and explain that she can use it to make a "kite." Let her use an eyedropper or a small spoon to place drops of tempera paint on one of the shape halves. Show her how to refold the shape, rub over it with her hands, and then open the shape to reveal the designs she created. When the kite has dried, help your child glue on a piece of yarn for a kite string. Display her kite where everyone can admire it.

A diamond shape becomes a familiar object in this art activity.

You Will Need

- ❑ white paper
- ❑ scissors
- ❑ ruler
- ❑ eye dropper or small spoon
- ❑ tempera paint
- ❑ glue
- ❑ yarn

Heart Lineup

Easy-to-make heart shapes are the game pieces in this learning activity.

You Will Need

- ❑ construction paper
- ❑ scissors
- ❑ large envelope

From construction paper, cut out six to eight hearts ranging in size from small to large. Mix up the shapes and spread them out on the floor. Talk with your child about the different sizes of the hearts, pointing out that they are all the same shape. Invite him to arrange the hearts in order from small to large. Together, count the number of hearts. then mix up the shapes, spread them out again, and encourage your child to arrange them in order from large to small. Keep the hearts stored in a large envelope for your child to play with again whenever he wishes.

Half Hearts, Whole Hearts

Cut five or six identical hearts, about 3 inches tall, out of different colors of construction paper. Give the hearts to your child and talk about their shape. Show her how to cut each one in half. Ask her to mix up the heart halves and place them in a pile. Give her a piece of white construction paper and some glue. Then invite her to put her matching-colored heart halves together and glue them onto her paper to create whole hearts.

Your child helps to make this fun heart-matching game.

You Will Need

- ❑ child-safe scissors
- ❑ ruler
- ❑ various colors of construction paper
- ❑ white construction paper
- ❑ glue

Star Counters

You can also make this number game with star stickers.

You Will Need

- ❑ index cards
- ❑ marker
- ❑ ink pad
- ❑ star-shaped rubber stamp
- ❑ envelope

Collect five index cards and use a marker to number them from 1 to 5. Sit with your child and set out the cards along with an ink pad and a star-shaped rubber stamp. Together, talk about the shape of the stamp and count the number of points the star has. Select a card and help your child name the numeral on it. Then invite him to stamp that number of star prints on the card. Continue in the same manner with the remaining cards. Let your child store the cards in an envelope. To play with his counters, have him remove one card at a time, name the numeral on it, and then count the accompanying number of star prints.

Stars Galore

Cut a large star shape out of construction paper. Show the star to your child and talk with her about its shape. How many points does the star have? Give your child a sheet of star stickers and show her how to remove the stickers one by one. Let her use the stickers to decorate her large star shape any way she wishes. Encourage her to continue until all the stickers on the sheet have been used.

For More Fun: When the star sticker sheet is empty, let your child place it under a piece of thin paper and color over it with the side of a crayon to make star rubbings.

This art activity encourages recognition of the star shape.

You Will Need

- ❑ scissors
- ❑ construction paper
- ❑ star stickers

Point and Name

You can play this language game with your child whenever you have a free minute.

You Will Need

❑ magazine or storybook

With your child, find a magazine or a storybook to look at together. Choose a shape, such as a circle, and talk with him about what the shape looks like. As you turn the pages of the magazine or book, help your child point to and name circular objects he sees in the pictures. Then choose another shape, such as a square, a triangle, a rectangle, or an oval, and play the game again.

Shape Books

Choose a shape such as a square. Make a blank book for your child by stacking several pieces of construction paper, cutting them into a square shape, and then stapling them together down the left-hand side. Print "My Square Book" and your child's name on the front. With your child, look through old magazines to find pictures of things that are square. Cut out the pictures and place them in a box. Give your child the book and the pictures, and talk with her about their square shapes. Then invite her to glue the pictures onto the pages of her book. Later, help your child make books for other shapes, such as a circle, a triangle, or a rectangle, and encourage her to "read" her books to you.

Your child will feel proud of making books that she can "read" to others.

You Will Need

- ❑ construction paper
- ❑ scissors
- ❑ stapler
- ❑ pen
- ❑ old magazines
- ❑ box
- ❑ glue

Shape Stencils

This art activity will keep your child busy while he has fun with basic shapes.

You Will Need

- ❑ plastic lids
- ❑ scissors
- ❑ craft knife
- ❑ paper
- ❑ crayons

Collect several plastic lids and use scissors to trim off the rims. Turn each lid into a stencil by using a craft knife to cut a basic shape, such as a circle, a square, a triangle, or a rectangle, out of the center. Set out paper and crayons and give your child the stencils. Talk with him about the cut-out shape in each one. Then let him place the lids on the paper and use crayons to trace around the edges of the shapes. Encourage him to move the stencils around and make several tracings of each one, overlapping the shapes and using different colors of crayons as he works. Let him continue as long as he likes.

Lick-and-Stick Shapes

In a small, disposable container, combine two parts washable white glue with one part white vinegar. Use a foam paintbrush to cover the back side of pieces of colored construction paper with the mixture. When the glue mixture has dried, apply a second coat. Allow the papers to dry again. Turn the papers over and draw on shapes such as circles, squares, triangles, rectangles, ovals, diamonds, hearts, and stars. Cut out the shapes. Then give them to your child to lick and stick on white paper any way she wishes. When she has finished, encourage her to point to and name the different shape stickers she used.

Homemade stickers make this art activity especially fun to do.

You Will Need

- ❑ disposable container
- ❑ washable white glue
- ❑ white vinegar
- ❑ foam paintbrush
- ❑ colored construction paper
- ❑ pen
- ❑ scissors
- ❑ white paper

Jeweled Crown

Basic shapes cut from colorful paper make perfect "jewels" for decorating a child's royal crown.

You Will Need

- ❑ construction paper
- ❑ pen
- ❑ scissors
- ❑ tape
- ❑ colorful paper
- ❑ aluminum foil
- ❑ glue

Use this easy method to make a crown for your child. Select a piece of construction paper. Draw a zigzag line lengthwise down the center of the paper and cut the paper in half along the line. Tape the ends of the two halves together to complete the crown, adjusting it as needed to fit your child's head. From colorful paper, such as construction paper or shiny gift-wrap, cut out small circles, squares, and triangles for jewels. Also cut a few diamond shapes out of aluminum foil. Then give the shapes to your child and let him glue them all over his crown for decorations.

Lacing Shape Cards

On a piece of lightweight cardboard or an old file folder, draw a 6- to 7-inch shape, such as a circle, a square, or a triangle, and cut it out. Use a hole punch to make holes about 1½ inches apart around the edge of the shape. Cut a piece of yarn about 2½ feet long. Tie one end of the yarn piece to one of the holes and wrap tape around the other end to make a "needle." Show your child how to lace the yarn around the edges of the shape, passing it in and out of the holes. When she has finished, trim the loose end of the yarn and tape it to the back of the shape. Make as many different Lacing Shape Cards for your child as you wish.

This art activity provides a great way to promote shape recognition.

You Will Need

- ❑ lightweight cardboard or file folder
- ❑ pen
- ❑ ruler
- ❑ scissors
- ❑ hole punch
- ❑ yarn
- ❑ tape

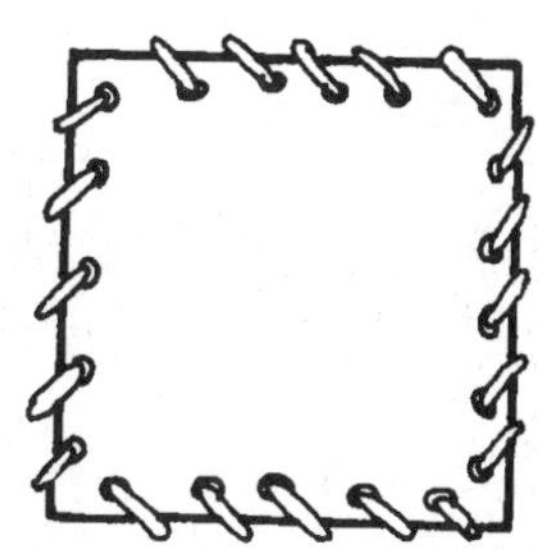

Shape Rubbings

With this art activity, your child sees shapes appear on his paper as if by magic.

You Will Need

- ❑ index cards or file folder
- ❑ scissors
- ❑ masking tape
- ❑ lightweight white paper
- ❑ old crayons

From index cards or an old file folder, cut out several shapes such as a circle, a square, a triangle, and a heart. Attach the shapes to a tabletop with loops of masking tape rolled sticky side out. Provide your child with lightweight white paper, such as computer paper, and old crayons with the papers removed. Help him place a piece of the paper on top of the shapes on the table. Then show him how to rub over the shapes with the side of a crayon to make the shape outlines "magically" appear. Can your child name each of the shapes? Encourage him to move his paper around and rub over the shapes again using a different color of crayon. Let him continue the activity as long as he likes.

Shape Pictures

Select several different colors of construction paper. Draw on various sizes of shapes such as circles, squares, triangles, rectangles, and ovals. Cut out the shapes and place them in a box. Set out white paper and glue. Sit with your child and show her how to take colored shapes from the box and arrange them on the white paper to make a picture of something such as a robot, a truck, or a house. Then invite her to choose shapes and arrange them any way she wishes to create her own "picture" or design. When she is satisfied with her arrangement, show her how to glue the shapes in place on her paper. Let her continue making other pictures with the remaining shapes, if she wishes.

Your child is sure to enjoy creating her own pictures with colorful shapes.

You Will Need

- ❑ colored construction paper
- ❑ pen
- ❑ scissors
- ❑ box
- ❑ white paper
- ❑ glue

Tear-and-Glue Shapes

This art activity promotes small-muscle development while reinforcing shape recognition.

You Will Need

- ❑ white construction paper
- ❑ pen
- ❑ colored construction-paper scraps
- ❑ glue
- ❑ yarn
- ❑ child-safe scissors

On a piece of white construction paper, draw a large shape such as a circle, a square, or a triangle. Give your child the paper along with colored construction-paper scraps and some glue. Show him how to tear the scraps into small pieces. Then invite him to glue the pieces all over the shape on his paper, covering it as completely as he can. When he has finished, give him a long piece of yarn. Help him glue it around the edges of the shape to make an outline, trimming off any excess yarn as necessary. Repeat the activity at other times with different shapes.

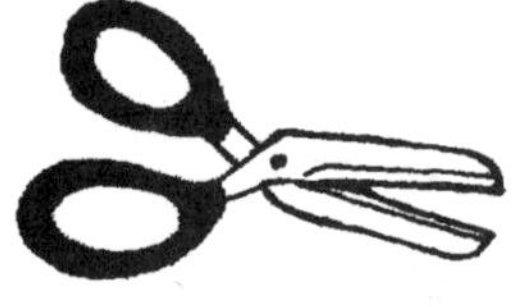

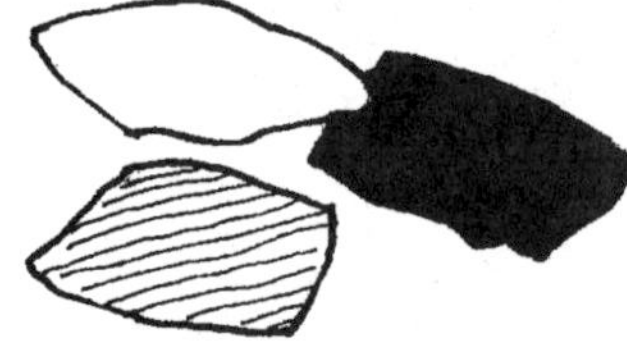

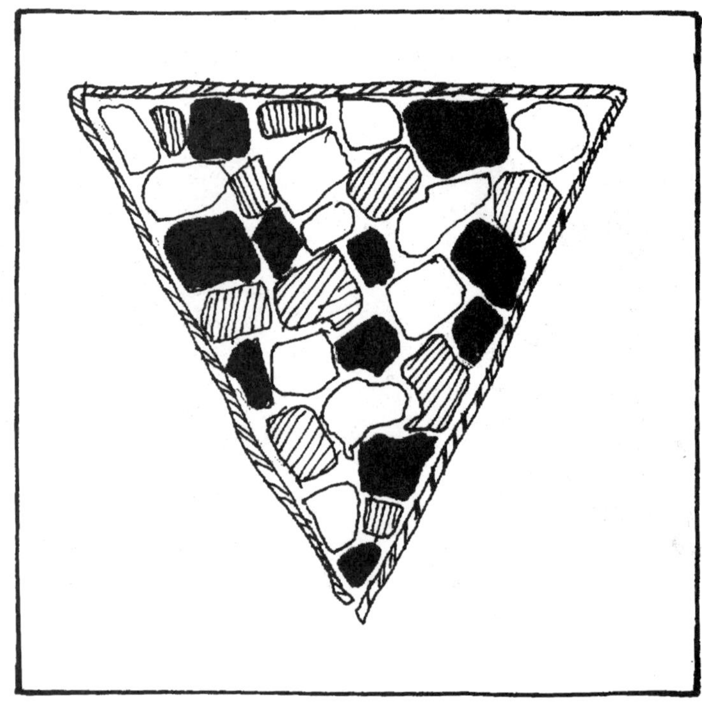

Shape Folder

On one color of construction paper, draw eight 3-inch shapes: a circle, a square, a triangle, a rectangle, an oval, a diamond, a heart, and a star. Cut out the shapes and place them on the inside halves of a file folder in any order you wish. Use a pen to trace around each shape. Then remove the shapes and store them in an envelope taped to the back of the file folder. To play, give your child the open file folder and the paper shapes. Invite her to choose one of the shapes and help her name it. Then ask her to place the shape on the matching-shaped outline on the file folder. Continue in the same manner with the remaining shapes.

Your child can play with this homemade shape-matching game as often as she likes.

You Will Need

- ❑ construction paper
- ❑ pen
- ❑ ruler
- ❑ scissors
- ❑ file folder
- ❑ envelope
- ❑ tape

Shape Concentration

Your child might want to invite other family members to join in this shape-recognition card game.

You Will Need

- ❑ small index cards
- ❑ crayon or marker

Select ten small index cards and divide them into five pairs. On each pair, use a crayon or a marker to draw a different shape, such as a circle, a square, a triangle, a rectangle, and a heart. Mix up the cards and spread them out facedown on the floor or on a table. Let your child begin by turning up two cards. If the shapes on the cards match, let him keep the cards. If the shapes don't match, ask him to replace both cards facedown exactly where they were before. Then you take a turn. Continue to play the game in the same manner until all the cards have been matched. The player who ends up with the most cards gets the first turn when you start the game again.

For Older Kids: Make the game more challenging by including pairs of cards for two or three more shapes.

Shape Sticks

Turn a shoebox upside down. Use a craft knife to cut two parallel rows of five slits each in the bottom of the box. Make each slit about 3/4 inch long. Collect ten large craft sticks and divide them into five pairs. On each pair, use a marker to draw a different shape, such as a circle, a square, a triangle, a rectangle, and a star. Insert one of the sets of sticks in one of the rows of slits in the shoebox. Then give the other set of sticks to your child and encourage her to insert the sticks with matching shapes in the appropriate slits in the other row. Later, remove the sticks, mix them up, and show your child how to insert the matching pairs of sticks into the slits by herself.

The sticks for this shape-matching game can be stored in the box your child uses for playing the game.

You Will Need

- ❑ shoebox
- ❑ craft knife
- ❑ ruler
- ❑ large craft sticks
- ❑ marker

Shape Sort

This sorting game helps your child see that a shape can come in a variety of colors.

You Will Need

- ❑ three colors of construction paper
- ❑ pen
- ❑ ruler
- ❑ scissors
- ❑ envelope

Select three pieces of construction paper in different colors. On each color of paper, draw four 3-inch shapes: a circle, a square, a triangle, and a rectangle. Cut out the shapes and mix them up. Then invite your child to sort the shapes into piles of circles, squares, triangles, and rectangles. Store the shapes in an envelope for him to play with again whenever he wishes.

For Older Kids: Start with four or five different-colored pieces of construction paper.

Dot-to-Dot Shapes

On a piece of paper, use a pen to draw a dot outline of a triangle or other shape. Give the paper to your child and talk with her about the shape of the outline. Then invite her to use a crayon or a pencil to connect the dots to complete the triangle. Let her decorate the triangle with crayon or pencil designs. Then draw a dot outline of a different shape for her to complete. Continue as long as interest lasts.

This shape-recognition activity is a great waiting game.

You Will Need

- ❑ paper
- ❑ pen
- ❑ crayon or pencil

Shape Patterns

You can also use shapes cut from construction paper to play this fun patterning game.

You Will Need

- ❑ two shapes of color code stickers
- ❑ lined paper

Purchase small color code stickers (available where office supplies are sold) in two different shapes, such as circles and rectangles. Sit with your child at a table, show him the stickers, and talk with him about their shapes. At the top of a piece of lined paper, attach several of the stickers in a simple pattern, such as circle-rectangle, circle-rectangle. Show your child how to use more of the stickers to copy the pattern on a line under your pattern. When he has become familiar with the game, give him other patterns to copy, such as circle-circle-rectangle, circle-circle-rectangle; or, circle-rectangle-rectangle-circle, circle-rectangle-rectangle-circle.

Touch and Guess

With a pencil, draw a square or other shape on a piece of lightweight paper, such as computer paper. Place the paper on a side of a cardboard carton and use the pencil point to punch holes around the outline of the shape. Make similar textured outlines of other shapes on other pieces of paper. Sit with your child at a table and ask her to close her eyes. Place one of the papers, textured side up, in front of her. Invite her to try to identify the shape on it by touching the textured outline with her hands and fingers. When she has done so, let her try to identify the shapes on the other papers in the same way. Store the papers in a large envelope for your child to play with again later, if you wish.

Your child uses the sense of touch to play this shape-recognition game.

You Will Need

- ❑ pencil
- ❑ lightweight paper
- ❑ cardboard carton
- ❑ envelope (optional)

Shape Board Game

This shape-recognition game is fun to play with two or three people.

You Will Need

- ❑ large piece of construction paper or cardboard
- ❑ marker
- ❑ index cards
- ❑ game markers

Select a large piece of construction paper or cardboard to use for making a gameboard. In the upper left-hand corner of the board, draw a circle and print *Start* inside of it. Then draw a pathway of circles, squares, triangles, and hearts in random order, winding back and forth down the paper. End with a circle in the lower right-hand corner and print *Finish* inside of it. Collect three or four small index cards for each shape and draw that shape on the cards. Mix up the cards and put them together in a deck facedown. Provide different kinds of game markers, such as a penny and a small eraser, for yourself and your child and place them on *Start.* To play, take turns choosing a card and moving your game marker to the next shape on the pathway that matches the shape on the card. Continue until both of you have reached the end of the path. Then let the person who finished first start the next round of the game.

Shapes All Around

When you and your child are going about your daily routines—whether indoors or out on errands—lead her to discover basic shapes in everyday items she sees around her. Below are just a few examples to get you started.

- Shapes of tabletops, couch cushions, pillows, rugs, books, and magazines
- Shapes of walls, doors, doorknobs, windows, and wall posters or paintings
- Shapes of bath towels, washcloths, sheets, pillow cases, and blankets
- Shapes in fabric patterns of clothing, furniture, curtains, and placemats
- Shapes in patterns of linoleum, carpets, wallpaper, and wall tiles
- Shapes in sidewalks, house fronts, road signs, and billboards

One of the easiest ways to teach shape recognition is to use everyday items around you.

You Will Need

❑ everyday items

Little Shapes

Your child is sure to have fun playing this musical shape-recognition game with you.

You Will Need

- ❑ construction paper
- ❑ scissors

From construction paper, cut out two each of several shapes, such as circles, squares, triangles, rectangles, and diamonds. Ask your child to help you lay the shapes out on the floor. Then sing the song below and have him do the actions with you, as indicated. Continue singing the song until you have picked up all the shapes.

Shapes on the Floor

Sung to: "Clementine"

Little shapes, little shapes,

Little shapes are on the floor.

I am picking up a circle.
(Pick up circle shape.)

See if you can find one more.
(Child picks up other circle shape.)

Repeat, each time substituting a different shape word for *circle*.

Elizabeth McKinnon

Shape Moves

Your child uses body movements to reinforce recognition of shapes.

You Will Need

❑ yarn

On a carpet, let your child help you make a large yarn outline of a shape such as a circle, a square, a triangle, or a rectangle. Invite her to move around the shape in various ways, such as crawling, hopping, tiptoeing, or walking heel-to-toe. Also encourage her to try walking around the shape backward, forward, and sideways, or like an animal such as a duck or an elephant. When the game is over, have her help you form a different shape and start all over again.

For More Fun: Use chalk to draw shapes outdoors on a sidewalk or a patio.

Mirror Shapes

Your child discovers how to make whole shapes out of halves with this science activity.

You Will Need

- ❑ small mirror with straight edge
- ❑ construction paper
- ❑ scissors

Find a small mirror with a straight edge, such as a compact mirror. From construction paper, cut out several small shapes, such as a circle, a square, a triangle, and a heart. Cut each shape in half. Sit with your child at a table and give him one of the shape halves. Then let him experiment with holding the mirror next to the half shape to make the shape appear to be whole. Continue in the same manner with the remaining shape halves.

Sunshine Shapes

From index cards or an old file folder, cut out several shapes, such as a circle, a square, a triangle, and a heart. Help your child attach the shapes to a piece of dark-colored construction paper, using loops of masking tape rolled sticky side out. Together, place the paper in direct sunlight and leave it there all day, if possible. Can your child predict what will happen to the paper as the sun shines on it? At the end of the day (or after at least several hours), let her remove the cut-out shapes from the paper. Which parts of the paper are the darkest? Which are the lightest? Why? (The parts that were covered by the cut-out shapes are the darkest because the sunlight shining on the other parts of the paper bleached out some of the color.)

This science activity is fun to do outside on a sunny day.

You Will Need

- ❑ index cards or file folder
- ❑ scissors
- ❑ dark-colored construction paper
- ❑ masking tape
- ❑ sunlight

Cracker Snacks

Crackers are great to use at snacktime for building shape-recognition skills.

You Will Need

- ❑ various shapes of crackers
- ❑ plate
- ❑ knife
- ❑ cheese slices

At snacktime, review basic shapes by placing various shapes of crackers—round, square, triangular, and rectangular—on a plate. Use a knife to cut matching shapes out of cheese slices and put them on the plate also. Talk with your child about the various shapes. Then invite him to place the cheese shapes on top of the matching-shaped crackers before eating.

Cookie Fun

Your entire family will love the results of this shape-recognition baking activity.

Purchase or make sugar cookie dough and roll it out as directed. Use a knife to cut out squares, triangles, rectangles, and diamonds. Let your child help cut out circles with the rim of a drinking glass, and ovals with the rim of a small tin can bent into an oval shape. Also let her help cut out heart and star shapes with cookie cutters, if available. Place the cookies on a baking sheet and bake according to the recipe directions. When the cookies have cooled, invite your child to help decorate them with frosting and sprinkles. Talk with her about the different cookie shapes as you work. Then serve and enjoy

You Will Need

- ❑ sugar cookie dough
- ❑ rolling pin
- ❑ knife
- ❑ drinking glass
- ❑ small tin can
- ❑ heart and star cookie cutters (optional)
- ❑ baking sheet
- ❑ frosting
- ❑ sprinkles

Parent Resources

from Totline® Publications

A Year of Fun

Hang up these age-specific resource guides for great advice on child development, practical parenting, and age-appropriate activities that jump-start learning.

- **Just for Babies**
- **Just for Ones**
- **Just for Twos**
- **Just for Threes**
- **Just for Fours**
- **Just for Fives**

Beginning Fun With Science

Make science fun for your child with these quick, safe, easy-to-do activities that lead to discovery and spark the imagination.

- **Bugs & Butterflies** • **Plants & Flowers**
- **Magnets** • **Rainbows & Colors**
- **Sand & Shells** • **Water & Bubbles**

Beginning Fun With Art

Perfect for introducing a young child to the fun of art while developing coordination skills and building self-confidence.

- **Scissors** • **Yarn** • **Paint** • **Modeling Dough**
- **Glue** • **Stickers** • **Craft Sticks** • **Crayons** • **Felt**
- **Paper Shapes** • **Rubber Stamps** • **Tissue Paper**

Learning Everywhere

These books present ideas for turning ordinary moments into teaching opportunities. You'll find ways to spend fun, quality time with your child while you lay the foundation for language, art, science, math, problem solving, and building self-esteem.

- **Teaching House**
- **Teaching Town**
- **Teaching Trips**

Getting Ready for School

Help your child develop the skills necessary for school success. These activity ideas combine ordinary materials with simple instructions for fun at home that leads to learning.

- **Ready to Learn Colors, Shapes, and Numbers**
- **Ready to Write and Develop Motor Skills**
- **Ready to Read** • **Ready to Communicate**
- **Ready to Listen and Explore the Senses**

Totline books and resources are available at fine teacher and parent stores.

Parent Resources

from Totline® Publications

Seeds for Success

Ideas on how to plant the seeds for success in young children. These parent-friendly books help encourage the development of creativity, responsibility, critical thinking, happiness, and good health. For ages 3 to 5.

- **Growing Creative Kids**
- **Growing Responsible Kids**
- **Growing Happy Kids**
- **Growing Thinking Kids**

Time to Learn

Now's the time for hands-on learning. Find out how to use low- and no-cost materials to effectively and simply teach your child at home.

- **Colors • Letters**
- **Measuring • Numbers**
- **Science • Shapes**
- **Matching and Sorting**
- **New Words**
- **Cutting and Pasting**
- **Drawing and Writing**
- **Listening**
- **Taking Care of Myself**

Learn With Piggyback Songs

Children will love to learn age-appropriate themes through music and movement with these delightful song books. Each book has 40 joyful songs and rhymes that help children learn about a specific topic. Plus developmentally appropriate activity ideas extend the learning fun!

- **Songs and Games for Babies**
- **Songs and Games for Toddlers**
- **Songs and Games for Threes**
- **Songs and Games for Fours**
- **Sing a Song of Letters**
- **Sing a Song of Animals**
- **Sing a Song of Colors**
- **Sing a Song of Holidays**
- **Sing a Song of Me**
- **Sing a Song of Nature**
- **Sing a Song of Numbers**
- **Sing a Song of Shapes**

Cassette Tapes

Cassette tapes, featuring selected songs from some of the Learn with Piggyback Songs books, include:

- **Songs for Babies**
- **Songs for Toddlers**
- **Songs for Threes**
- **Songs for Fours**

Totline books and resources are available at fine teacher and parent stores.